Tragedy

4

lov - in' you._____ Tra - ge - dy. When the

feel - in's gone and you can't go on it's tra - ge - dy. When the morn - in' cries and you don't know why. It's

hard to __ bear. __ With no one to love you you're go - in' no - where.

Tra - ge - dy. When you lose con - trol and you got no soul it's tra - ge - dy.

When the

6

S. A.

hard to bear._____ With no one to love you you're go-in' no-where. _Ba ya_____

_ba ya_____ go-in' no-where. _Ba ya_____

_ba ya_____ Tra-ge-dy.

It's raining men

Paul Jabara and Paul Schaffer
arr. Charles Beale

14

Y. M. C. A.

Jacques Morali, Henri Belolo and Victor Willis
arr. Charles Beale

OPTIONAL DISCO PERCUSSION BREAK
REPEAT AD LIB (AT LEAST THREE TIMES), ADDING YOUR OWN SOUNDS AND PATTERNS.
CLAP ON BEATS 2 AND 4. INVENT YOUR OWN DANCE ROUTINE IF YOU LIKE.

22